DUPLEIX

AND THE

EMPIRE OF INDIA

DUPLEIX

AND THE

EMPIRE OF INDIA

KSIDNEY J. OWAN

GYAN

Published by

GYAN

Gyan Publishing House
5, Ansari Road
Daryaganj, New Delhi-110002
Phone: 011-47034999, 9811692060
E-mail: books@gyanbooks.com

Distribution Network
gyanbooks.com
India, USA, Canada, UK, Australia

ISBN: 978-93-6433-268-2 (PB)

First Published, 1887

2nd Impression 2024

Printed at: Gyan Press, Delhi.

DUPLEIX AND THE EMPIRE OF INDIA
Author: SIDNEY J. OWAN

DUPLEIX

AND THE

EMPIRE of INDIA

BY

SIDNEY J. OWEN.

NEW YORK:
JOHN B. ALDEN, PUBLISHER.
1887.

DUPLEIX

AND

The Indian Empire.

The military adventurer has, in all ages, been a prominent figure in India; and history of that country derives much of its interest from the remarkable characters and brilliant achievements of such men, and their commanding influence on the fortunes of a community discordant in race, national sentiment, and religion, weak in political institutions and public spirit, and hence peculiarly liable to revolutions wrought out by the sword. Thus, without citing earlier instances, the Mogul empire was founded, undermined and laid low by three representatives of this class, each well suited to his mission, and all memorable for the wild romance of their exploits. The quick-witted, large-hearted, and enlightened Baber, a conqueror in his boyhood, youthful in spirit to the end, a knight-errant ever, was happily adapted to conciliate his Indian subjects; and to stamp upon the government of his new dominions that blended character of energy and tolerance, which it long retained under his descendants, and which contributed so much to its stability. But when the gloomy and persecuting Aurungzib laid his hand heavily on the Hindoos, Sivaji arose as their deliverer and avenger: his subtlety, political ability, skill in irregular warfare, religious zeal, and national spirit, made him irrepressible, and the Hindoo reaction, initiated by him, irresistible. Sapped by the Mahrattas, the tottering empire was prostrated by Nadir Shah. This grim, inflexible, and able soldier, who freed Persia from a foreign yoke only to usurp the throne, enforce a change of religion, play the tyrant, and perpetrate frantic cruelties which cost him his life, was an appropriate instrument for the repetition of Timour's work of destruction; and Nadir's indiscriminate massacre at Delhi recalled the dread memory of "the Scourge of God."

The fortunes of the Anglo-Indian empire have been not less notably affected by the same class of men, though hitherto the general results of their operations have been favorable to it. The enterprise of adventurers called it into being, precipitated its development, and gave occasion to each great step in its advance. Dupleix's policy forced the Madras government to take up Mahomed Ali's cause; Clive, the "heaven-born general," sustained it; and the relation thus established inevitably ended in the British annexation of the Carnatic. Anaverdy Khan made himself master of the Bengal provinces; and though he refused to quarrel with the English, his fatuous partiality for Surajah Dowlah brought about the crisis which he deprecated. Plassey was the *contre-coup* of the attack on Calcutta. The rise of Hyder, and the close alliance of his house with the French, led eventually to the British conquest of Mysore. De Boigne made Mahadajee Sindia predominant at D.lhi, and over a great part of Hindostan, though both he and his patron were careful to keep on good terms with the English. But when another soldier of fortune, Ameer Khan, incited Jeswunt Roa Holka-, an adventurer like himself, to march on Poona, the defeated Peishwa fled to Bombay, and concluded the treaty of Bassein. This Mahadajee's successor, proud of the position won for him by De Boigne, and relying on the powerful army which the Savoyard had organized, thought proper to oppugn; and the triumphant English mulcted him of the so-called north-west provinces. In the ebb tide of British policy, after Wellesley's departure, Ameer Khan prepared the way for new annexations, both by exhibiting in his own licentious proceedings the intolerable evils attending non-intervention, and by stimulating the growth of a yet more debased type of adventurers, the Pindaris, for whose suppression forces were assembled by Lord Hastings. This circumstance hastened the intriguing and suspicious Peishwa's explosion; and his defeat, surrender, and deposition transferred his dominions to the company. In Wellesley's days, an Irish sailor, George Thomas, had made himself independent on the borders of the Indian desert; had played a masterful part in the Cis-Sutlej Sikh country; and had projected the conquest of the Punjab and of Sinde. He was cut off before he could attempt either object; and Runjit Singh united and disciplined the northern Sikhs, and maintained a dubious faith with the English. But the proud and adventurous spirit which he had strengthened in his army impelled it, on his death, to cross the Sikh Rubicon; and the Punjab soon became British territory. It must be added that one view of the conquest of Sinde would represent Sir Charles

Napier as a predetermined military adventurer. Of the names we have mentioned, some are absolutely unknown, others little more than names, to most Englishmen. But of Dupleix's ambition, vanity, sudden elevation, equally sudden reverses, who has not read in the fascinating pages of Macaulay? Yet, as Mr. Justice Stephen has lately shown, Macaulay is an unsafe guide to truth in Indian history. And there is special ground for distrusting his account of Clive's great rival. His essay was written *à propos* of Sir John Malcolm's *Life of Clive.* But Malcolm contributes no original information on Dupleix and his proceedings. He dispatches in a few lines, in accordance with Orme's narrative, the story of the surrender of Madras, and Dupleix's breach of the capitulation, while he fills twenty-four pages, describing Clive's defence of Arcot, with a quotation from Orme. That writer is evidently both his authority and Macaulay's at this period. But Orme, admirable historian as he is in general, was imperfectly acquainted with Dupleix, and much prejudiced against him. As a personal friend of Clive, who broke his *parole* on the faith of Labourdonnais's version of the occasion and merits of his quarrel with Dupleix,

Orme would be inclined to misjudge the French governor-general from the outset; and Dupleix's later conduct did not tend to remove the impression of perfidy, usurped authority, and extreme arrogance thus associated with his name. Hence he became in Orme's eyes, in spite of his ability and perseverance, both odious and contemptible. It must be remembered also that, while Labourdonnais was indefatigable in circulating his own story, Dupleix's lips were sealed by authority, when he undertook to vindicate his career, and press his claims on the French East India Company. Thus he says:

> Le sieur Dupleix respecte trop les ordres du ministère et ceux de la compagnie pour oser publier ici ce qu'il lui a été enjoint d'ensevelir dans le plus profond secret, et, quelqu 'intérêt qu'il puisse avoir de justifier une conduite qu'il n'ignore pas que beaucoup de personnes ont condamnée, ce motif, tout puissant qu'il est, cédera toujours à la loi du devoir.

Thus Dupleix continued to be misunderstood and underrated; and Macaulay, by a few vigorous and confident strokes, from an unfavorable portrait produced a caricature of the real man. An anonymous writer in the defunct *National Review* (October, 1862) first as far as we are aware, explained the true state of the case relative to Madras and its treatment by the rival French officers; and later still Colonel Malleson in his *History of the French in India* has done ample justice to Dupleix. But the interest of the subject is by no means exhausted. Much of Dupleix's voluminous correspondence still awaits publication. A recent French writer, M. Tibulle Hamont, has consulted this, and based upon it a detailed and enthusiastic biography, interspersed with copious extracts from the letters, which throw a new and vivid light on the character and conduct of the brilliant adventurer.

M. Hamont is not free from the *lues Boswelliana;* and we are often quite unable to sympathize with his reflections, or to admit the force of his reasoning and the soundness of his conclusions. But his contribution to the knowledge of his hero's personality seems to us a really valuable one; and with the advantage of this fresh illustration we propose to give a short outline of the critical passages in Dupleix's career, and to attempt to appreciate fairly his character, designs, and achievements. Whatever his faults, he certainly deserves a better fate than to be held up to scorn as a clever, but vain-glorious and detected charlatan.

François Joseph Dupleix was born on the first day of the year 1697, at Landrecies. His father was a farmer-general of taxes, apparently a narrow-minded and austere money-maker, and a stern despot in the family circle, whose constant aim was to make his son a thorough, but a mere, man of business, rigidly proscribing all higher culture, and especially all scope for the imagination. But the exclusive side of this policy defeated itself. As so often happens in similar cases, the forbidden fruit was eagerly snatched by the boy, who was of a dreamy and enthusiastic temperament; and he soon reveled in the world of ideas, and devoted himself to studies very remote from bookkeeping, including that of music, which throughout his career was his solace, and in some sense his inspirer. He combined with a love of the fine arts a taste for the severer studies of mathematics and fortification. His father was naturally much provoked: *Passe encore pour les mathématiques*, he exclaimed indignantly, *mais la fortification et le reste!* Such perversity required sharp discipline; and in 1715, that is at the age of eighteen, the youth was sent to sea on board of an East-Indiaman. From his voyages he returned with much information, and what the domestic oracle considered sound ideas on trade and maritime affairs.

Being a large shareholder in the French East India Company, the elder Dupleix, in 1720, procured for his son a seat in the Council at Pondicherry, with the then almost nominal and ill-paid, but to Dupleix very suggestive, post of *commissaire des guerres.* Lenoir, the governor of Pondicherry, was a shrewd and kindly man, well versed in Indian politics: he quickly discerned the capacity of the young councilor, and employed him in a manner well adapted to prepare him for his enterprising career. Under Lenoir's tuition, Dupleix explored the archives of the company, and was intrusted with the drafting of dispatches to France and the native powers.

It soon appeared that, whatever his original tastes, his commercial training had not been thrown away. The company's commerce was in a very bad state. The most elementary principles of political economy were ignored by the professed men of business; and it was reserved for the votary of the muses to work out a salutary reform by the application of those principles. The commercial agents, both at Pondicherry and in Europe, were content to purchase Indian goods with French gold, and neglected both the introduction of western commodities into India, and a similar traffic with the outlying regions of Asia. Hence their operations were comparatively feeble and intermittent, and their profits very small. But the company's servants were not forbidden to trade, on their own account, with the interior of the country. Dupleix availed himself of this opening; obtained much money in return for the European goods in which he speculated; and induced his father to engage in an enterprise that gave him the double satisfaction of receiving a good dividend, and feeling that his son was, on one side of his character at least, a chip of the old block.

For several years Dupleix continued thus to amass wealth, and made comprehensive studies of the political situation; though it may be doubted whether, as M. Hamont asserts, he was already dreaming of the conquest of India; the rather, as no passage is cited in proof of this precocious reverie. In 1730 he was appointed governor of Chandernagore in Bengal. This settlement was in a more dilapidated condition than Pondicherry. But it was a sphere that suited him; and his influence was soon marvelously displayed in the development of its commercial activity. The place was well situated both for internal and foreign traffic; and the example of the new governor's profitable enterprise in purchasing vessels and goods, and pushing them seaward to remote Asiatic ports, and along the great river highways far up the country, stimulated the settlers, whom he freely assisted with his capital, and so effectually, that at the end of ten years French wares supplied many of the great cities of Hindostan, and were even sent up to Thibet; Chandernagore mustered, instead of five, not less than seventy-two ships engaged in the carrying trade with western India, Arabia, and China; and the increasing opulence of the place is said to have been attested by the construction of ten thousand new houses.

In 1741 the governor married a remarkable woman, whose influence on his career was destined to be very great. She was a widow: her father was French, her mother an Indo-Portuguese, and a scion of the historic house of De Castro. Madame Dupleix was born and educated in India. Her manners are said to have been fascinating: her strength of character and intelligence, her diplomatic tact, and her proficiency in native languages, were notable, and invaluable to her husband, whose political designs, if not suggested, were warmly embraced and actively promoted by her. A mutual and deep devotion, in weal and woe, seemed to have united the brilliant Frenchman and the accomplished Eurasian, not unlike that which existed later between Warren Hastings and *his* foreign wife.

The year of his marriage was also that of Dupleix's appointment as governor of Pondicherry, including the supreme control over the other French possessions, Chandernagore in Bengal, Karikal on the Coromandel, and Mahé on the Malabar coast. He was provided with a council of five members, who appear to have been throughout very submissive to his ascendency. The company nominated—and could recall—all these officers, though the royal sanction ratified the appointment, and supplemented it with a royal commission, and justice ran in the king's name. The powers of the governor-general were very extensive, but were conveyed in terms perhaps too indefinite. Each of the settlements had its governor and council, who were bound to obey the orders of the ruler of Pondicherry. This is not the occasion for tracing, even in outline, the previous history of the French East India Company. But it may be mentioned that it had already exhibited tendencies strictly analogous to those with which the student of our own company's annals is familiar. The directors limited their aspirations to a large dividend, and were most anxious to "keep a calm sough," and avoid any proceedings which might compromise their proper object, by involving them in local troubles. On the other hand, some of their governors had attained a dim consciousness that while their trade was by no means flourishing, it might prosper more if they secured a stronger footing in the country, and more commanding influence over the natives. Thus M. Dumas had already shown great resolution in resisting and defying Mahratta dictation. After Law's bubble had burst, the French government, and the French people generally, took little interest in Indian affairs.

Since the fusion of the rival companies in England our countrymen in the east had subsided into quiet traders, and had been much abler and more successful in their calling than their natural enemies the French. This once favorite phrase we use advisedly; for the petty jealousy of the commercial spirit, the close neighborhood of the French and English settlements on the Coromandel coast, the remoteness of the overruling authorities in Europe, and the circumstances that each settlement was fortified, and possessed the nucleus of an army, all tended to aggravate national antipathies, and to provoke collisions, which would have been more frequent but for the surviving respect for the native powers. If the emperor was a phantom, he was still an august phantom, and inspired fear. If the great subahdar of the Dekkan, Nizam ul Mulk, was afar off, he was well known to have long arms. And the nawab of the Carnatic at the time was not only his titular deputy, but had been actually selected and supported by him; and was moreover a man of character and vigor, with large military resources at his disposal. But Dupleix's bold spirit was not to be thus intimidated; and he early resolved to turn the imperial authority to his own account. It must be remembered that the practical dismemberment of the empire was almost complete; that the viceroy of the Dekkan, or India south of the Nerbudda, was virtually an independent sovereign, though the great Mahratta confederacy, of which the Peishwa was becoming the acknowledged head, was his constant and formidable rival; and that Mysore was still a comparatively insignificant state, under Hindoo rule, Hyder Ali being a young adventurer in the service of Nunjiraj, the *dulway* or regent of that kingdom.

Whatever might be his ulterior designs, Dupleix's immediate attention was engrossed by preparation for the impending war between his countrymen and the English, arising out of the disputed Austrian succession. His first step was characteristic. Knowing too well the feebleness of his military resources, and the precariousness of timely aid from beyond the sea, he sought to st engthen his political position in the eyes of the natives, which might be not less useful in the coming crisis than in the promotion of remoter schemes. His predecessor Dumas had obtained from the emperor, through the Mogul governor of the Carnatic, the title of nawab for himself and his official successors. This title Dupleix now assumed with much pomp, impressive to a native mind, ridiculous in the eyes of the French settlers, unaware of the serious object of the ceremony or sceptical of its advantages. He then repaired to Bengal, and there paraded his semi-barbaric grandeur, exchanging visits of state with the native governor of Hooglee, and exciting the same sensations as in the Carnatic. Thus, he flattered himself, he was regularly enrolled in the official hierarchy of the empire. He had, so to speak, taken up his native peerage.

On his return he devoted himself to the reduction of expenditure, the control of the civil functionaries, the increase, organization, and training of his little army, and the completion of the defences of Pondicherry. The chief defect of the works was, that as the citadel commanded the strand, there was no wall or ditch on that side. This deficiency he now supplied; and of this he was very proud, and laid great stress upon it in his *Mémoire*, as he was fully entitled to do; for it was a great and costly undertaking, and he both devised it, superintended its construction, and paid for it out of his own purse. But his labors were rudely interrupted. On 18th September, 1743, he received most discouraging and embarrassing orders from his employers. He was directed to retrench the expenditure by one-half, and to spend no more at present on fortification, although the same dispatch apprised him that war was almost certain. To obey such orders would have been fatal to French interests in India; to transgress them might be perilous to himself. In this cruel dilemma he chose a middle course—as before, at his own cost. He had already done his utmost to retrench ordinary expenditure, and had paid off most of the debt incurred on military preparation, when Pondicherry had been, a few years before, threatened by the Mahrattas. He now advanced out of his own funds 500,000 livres, one half of which he allotted to the defences, the other half to the freight of two vessels, which he dispatched with a justification of his proceedings, and an urgent petition for a military reinforcement and the aid of a fleet

After a tedious delay he received a disheartening reply. England and France were now at war; but instead of sending him soldiers, the directors recommended him to conclude a neutrality between the commercial settlements of the hostile nations. In case this should not be feasible, it was added, Labourdonnais, the governor of the Isles of France and of Bourbon, had been ordered to conduct a fleet to Pondicherry. Dupleix found, as he feared, that Mr. Morse, the governor of Fort St. George, would not consent to stand neutral: Pondicherry was almost defenceless: a large English fleet was cruising in the eastern seas; and the arrival of Labourdonnais was quite uncertain. In this emergency Dupleix's previous policy stood him in good stead. Reminding Anwarodeen, the Nawab of the Carnatic, of the long-standing friendship between the rulers of that province and the French, and of the Mogul dignity conferred upon M. Dumas and his successors, and denouncing Mr. Morse's turbulent disposition, he persuaded the Nawab to forbid an attack on Pondicherry by the English; who were however assured that if the French should become the stronger party a similar check should be placed upon them. Our countrymen as yet stood too much in awe of the Mogul power to disobey such a mandate. Dupleix meanwhile had dispatched his single vessel with a pressing request that Labourdonnais would hasten to his relief. That remarkable man made extraordinary exertions to replace the fleet of which he had been deprived. He detained, re-equipped, and armed for naval service every merchant ship that put in at the islands; mustered and trained every available man on the spot; levied an African force; displayed wonderful versatility in organizing every department of the armament, and in restoring its efficiency when impaired by a hurricane off Madagascar; fought an indecisive action with Admiral Peyton near Negapatam; and, the English fleet next day leaving the coast clear, made the best of his way to Pondicherry.

We now approach a passage in Dupleix's history which has been strangely misrepresented. Our countrymen at the time, piqued at the loss of Madras, blinded by national antipathy and personal prejudice against their ambitious and indómitable antagonist, flattered by the blandishments and misled by the sophistry of Labourdonnais, too readily accepted his statement of the case; even Orme afterward adopted it; and the traditional legend has since been stereotyped in Macaulay's celebrated essay on Clive.

The relations between the two distinguished men were, at first, most cordial. Dupleix's great objects were the defeat of the English fleet, and the capture of Madras. Labourdonnais professed strong sympathy, and stated that without the protection of a fleet Madras must fall easily. Dupleix reinforced his vessels with heavy guns; and by address and liberal gifts induced the nawab to withhold his promised protection from the English, who had solicited it too much as a matter of course, and empty-handed. But Labourdonnais now suggested that, on taking Madras, he should load his fleet with its merchandise, and restore the town to the enemy, on payment of a ransom. Here M. Hamont justly observes: *Cette manière d'envisager la question sentait plus le corsaire que l'homme d'état.* Dupleix naturally objected to this strange proposal, made at a time when England and France were at war, and so soon after the governor of Madras had refused to agree that the commercial settlements in India should remain neutral during the European contest. Without committing himself to a premature opinion as to the destiny of the town, he argued that it would be expedient, at any rate, to raze its fortifications.

From this time Labourdonnais seemed a changed man. Accustomed to command, he could not brook an equal, much less a superior; and he resented instructions, however gently communicated and reasonably justified. He grew sullen, captious, hesitating. He appeared more inclined to dispute than to act.

At length, the English fleet having fled disgracefully before him, he attacked Madras with his usual vigor, and it fell almost without resistance. On leaving Pondicherry, he had again harped on the restitution project, and had been answered decisively. Yet he now agreeed to a *conditional* capitulation in that sense: *Si par rachat ou rançon on remet la ville à MM. les Anglais*, etc. Still there was no positive engagement to that effect; though reporting that the capitulation left him free to choose between destroying the town, making it a French colony, or restoring it on ransom, he pronounced in favor of the third course. Dupleix informed him that, to prevent the Nawab yielding to the importunity of the English, he had been obliged to promise that the city should be given up to Anwarodeen, though he apparently intended first to destroy the fortifications. To this promised cession Labourdonnais assented. And the Governor-General in the interim made the victor governor, and sent a council to assist him, which was the usual plan on a new acquisition by the company. But this exercise of supreme authority Labourdonnais vehemently resented, and now announced that he *had* concluded a treaty for the ransom of the town. It is clear that, apart from the promise to the Nawab, he had no right whatever to do so. Indeed, he virtually admitted this later. But in vain Dupleix argued, entreated, appealed to the better nature of the stubborn and arrogant sailor. He only changed his line of defence, and in impudent disregard of facts declared himself pledged in honor to execute the treaty, in consequence of a promise which he had made at the time of the surrender, and to which he now ascribed his easy victory. He had been silent as to this promise at the time. The tone of his subsequent letters had belied it. It was not embodied in the capitulation. And it was certain that the place had been incapable of holding out. Yet upon this alleged secret compact he now took his stand resolutely, desperately. How is his conduct to be explained? Whatever his other motives, there is too good ground for suspecting, as was charged against him later in France, but could not be proved, that he had been bought by the English, who preferred afterward to enlarge on Dupleix's Punic faith, rather than to testify against the inveterate enemy of their great foe.

We must pass over the violent scenes that

ensued, and have only space to mention that Labourdonnais placed in arrest some of the commissioners sent by Dupleix to vindicate his authority, and the others fled.

The Governor-General was helpless, but his mutinous admiral was ill at ease, and tried to gain a legitmate standpoint by negotiating with his rival for a postponement of the restoration. Dupleix, reduced to extremity, and probably hoping to gain time until the admiral should be obliged to quit the coast, affected readiness to treat on this basis. But, pending the negotiation, a violent hurricane destroyed half of Labourdonnais's ships, and disabled the rest. He was now driven to resort to an audacious diplomatic *coup d'état.* He produced his treaty, asserted that it *had been* assented to at Pondicherry, executed it himself, procured it execution by the English—prisoners of war as they were:—and dispatching it to Dupleix, called upon him to abide by it. He soon after left India forever; and thenceforth maintained that *he* had acted loyally, and Dupleix perfidiously and tyrannically. Such is a bare but exact outline of this memorable quarrel. What Dupleix might have been tempted to do, but for the hurricane, is one thing. What he actually did, namely repudiate an unauthorized treaty, to which he was falsely asserted to have agreed, and the fundamental principle of which he had from the first opposed, is quite another thing. He was by no means scrupulous. But in this case he was certainly far more sinned against than sinning. Much doubt also hangs over the story of his ill-treatment of the English prisoners. Whether he meant originally to fulfill his promise of giving up Madras to the Nawab is doubtful. He perhaps intended, as we have intimated, to dismantle it, and then transfer it to Anwarodeen. But the dispute with the victor, and the impatience of the native ruler, prevented this. And, as Dupleix had predicted, the long and inevitable delay in the fulfilment of the promise, turned the Nawab into an enemy, and an ally of the English.

The position was now critical in the extreme. The French fleet had disappeared; the English fleet was intact, and threatened to return. The Nawab sent a considerable force to besiege Madras. To defend that city and Pondicherry only 2,000 Europeans and twice that number of sepoys were available. General despondency prevailed at the seat of government. But Dupleix saw clearly that the case was not hopeless. Some time must elapse before the enemy could muster and combine their armaments for a general attack. By a bold and sudden blow he might paralyze the Nawab, and perhaps force him again to change sides. For this purpose he selected Paradis, a veteran Swiss officer, whose capacity and energy he well knew, and detached him with 200 Europeans and 700 sepoys to attack the camp of Maphuz Khan, the Nawab's general, and eldest son. Meanwhile he still continued to negotiate with Anwarodeen. Eprémenil, the governor of Madras, was ordered to remain strictly on the defensive. The besiegers at first confined themselves to a close blockade; but after a while they diverted the river, and intercepted a spring which supplied the place with fresh water. These measures exasperated and alarmed the garrison. Dupleix saw that his hour was come, and insisted on a sortie. Four hundred men, with two field-pieces, sallied from the city, and were charged impetuously by a host of cavalry. But the swift fire of the field-pieces amazed, checked, and at the fourth discharge sent the horsemen to the right-about. The French sustained absolutely no loss. And Maphuz Khan, hearing that Paradis's relieving force was on the march, retired to St. Thomé, and encamped on the south bank of a river, confiding in its protection, and keeping a careless look-out. Dupleix planned an attack on this exposed position, to be made simultaneously by the Swiss and Eprémenil. Paradis suddenly appeared on the northern bank of the river; dashed across it, sword in hand, at the head of his men; and before the enemy could do much execution with their slow fire, fell upon them with the bayonet, and drove them before him in headlong flight into St. Thomé. Thence the dense mass of fugitives was quickly dislodged, only to be again assailed by the garrison of Madras: in wild panic they dispersed, and rushed onward toward Arcot.

These complete and startling victories are memorable to all time. They dispelled the awe of native authority, and proclaimed to all the world that the European was the destined successor of the proud Mogul and the fiery Mahratta.

Relieved from immediate anxiety on account of the Nawab, Dupleix next attempted the reduction of Fort St. David. A comparatively strong force was sent against it. But this, in deference to professional jealousy, was commanded by a very inferior officer. M. Bury's failure was as signal as Paradis's success. He posted his men in a walled garden, near the fort, and on the south side of the river. A sudden alarm in the night occasioned a panic; and instead of holding their own in so defensible a position, the troops rushed to the river, and crossed it in the face of the Nawab's arms. But for the field-pieces, which covered the crossing, a rout would have been inevitable, and the loss severe. Bury returned ingloriously to Pondicherry. But the glamour of the late victories was not dispelled by this reverse; and Dupleix's calculations were justified by a successful negotiation with the Nawab, who agreed to make peace, to abandon the English, and to cancel the bargain for the surrender of Madras. His son, Maphuz Khan, visited Pondicherry; was received with great honor, and loaded with presents, which, as the governor explained to his masters, were an excellent political investment. He then planned another assault on Fort St. David, and intrusted it to Paradis. But just as the gallant Swiss had reoccupied the walled garden, and was on the point of attacking, the English fleet was signaled, and he was fain to retreat.

Again the outlook was most gloomy; again

the civilians counseled surrender to inevitable fate. But Admiral Griffin confined himself to his own element; and Dupleix, having hastily summoned assistance from the French islands, was cheered by the arrival of some ships, which succeeded in reinforcing Madras with 300 men; but then, from fear of the English fleet, retired hastily. And tidings soon after arrived from Europe which might well appal even the Governor-General's stout heart. The most formidable flotilla which had ever appeared in the eastern waters was on its way, carrying a strong body of troops, and its commander, Admiral Boscawen, had it in charge to besiege Pondicherry. The directors exhorted their governor to make a good defence, but sent him no help of any kind. He resolved to attack Cuddalore, which lay over against Fort St. David, immediately, hoping, if successful, to impede the landing of the enemy there and to intercept their communication with the fort, or, more probably, to make Cuddalore a base for the capture of the fort itself. But Major Lawrence, who had lately arrived from England as commander of all the company's forces, defeated this movement by a simple stratagem. During the day, and in sight of the French, he removed the guns from Cuddalore, as if intent only on defending Fort St. David. But at nightfall he quietly replaced them; and the assailants were warmly received, and fled back in confusion to Pondicherry. Dupleix met them at the barriers, and was so deeply dejected at the reverse, that for one brief moment he meditated suicide. But a movement of his horse caused him to look up. The sight of the solid ramparts, surmounted by the proud banner of France, reassured him. And he resolved to live, and—if die he must—to die in the defence of his post.

At length the enemy appeared in overwhelming force, but not until the plan of the defence had been well considered and arranged. On the sea side, the town was protected by Dupleix's new wall and by shoal water. A bound hedge of prickly-pear made a bold circuit on the land side; and the advance of the besiegers to the Vaubanized walls was more effectually impeded by a chain of redoubts to the north and west, by Ariancopan, a fort on the south-west, and by an inlet of the sea or river of the same name to the south. Being well provided with artillery, Dupleix hoped to cope with, and even overpower, the enemy's batteries; and by sorties and skirmishes to harass the communications between the fleet and the English army, capture convoys, and obstruct the prosecution of the trenches. Then the monsoon might befriend him.

The admiral was commander-in-chief on land as well as at sea, a fact which must not be forgotten in estimating the result. The river was passed, not without an obstinate contest and serious casualties from the fire of the adjacent fort, a rash assault upon which was repulsed; and much valuable time was lost in besieging and afterward repairing it. It was stoutly defended; but a casual explosion having much reduced the number of the garrison, and spread panic among the survivors, this important position was evacuated. Thus the external line of defence was turned, and the other outworks became almost useless. But the English engineers were thoroughly incapable. By their advice, Boscawen opened his batteries at a distance far too great to be of any avail; and on pushing the trenches nearer, the ground was found to be hopelessly swampy and impracticable. Dupleix ordered a sally. But the state of the ground and other causes retarded the advance; and the English, well prepared, routed the assailants, killing many officers, among them Paradis. Still, in spite of this serious loss, and the partial demolition of the bastion which Boscawen had chosen as his objective, time went on, and the siege made little progress. The superiority of Dupleix's fire was pronounced; the damage to the bastion was rapidly repaired; and Madame Dupleix's secret relations with our native soldiers are said to have supplied information, which caused much mischief by facilitating attacks on convoys.

Foiled on land, the admiral ordered a general bombardment by the fleet. This lasted for twelve hours consecutively. Orme says that the only casualty it caused was the death of one old woman. The boisterous challenge, being found so ineffective, presently remained unanswered. But landward the French batteries replied vigorously, and overpowered those opposed to them. The monsoon was at hand; the mortality in the English army had been great; the health of the troops was failing; and it was high time for the fleet to seek safer anchorage. This place was too strong to be taken by a *coup de main*. Boscawen therefore suddenly broke up the siege, and retired; leaving to his antagonist the imperishable honor of having, with a very small force, and by his own engineering skill, baffled the most imposing European armament that had ever been engaged in Indian warfare.

Dupleix's exultation was, of course, great; and he announced his triumph far and wide to the native potentates, receiving in return the florid compliments which the Oriental is ever ready to bestow on such occasions. The peace of Aix-la-Chapelle soon after restored Madras to the English, and, however mortifying in this respect to the French Governor-General, left him free to prosecute his ambitious enterprises among the natives. But it must be remembered that the English set him an example by an armed intervention in Tanjore, which resulted in their acquisition of Devicottah, at the mouth of the Coleroon.

And here it is material to observe that it does not seem very clear when Dupleix first conceived the idea of subjecting the "country powers" to French ascendency; nor how far he was, in the first instance, prepared to soar even in his dreams of empire. His military and diplomatic success in dealing with Anwarodeen may have emboldened him to consider the Oriental as his convenient tool. His triumph over Boscawen not only elated him at the moment, but would be apt to make him miscalculate the force of English opposition to his designs. Chunda Sahib's overtures so exactly accorded with the train of political associations already raised in the case of Anwarodeen, that the temptation to accept them would be the stronger, especially when they included an offer of alliance with the pretender to the Dekkan subahdary, and thus promised to establish French influence on a legitimate basis over the greater portion of India south of the Nerbudda. He was doubtless much encouraged by the political hesitation of the English; and the more so as he probably did not fully appreciate the grounds of that hesitation, and attributed it too much to fear of his arms, and too little to the conviction that the English directors would be slow to sanction even defensive operations against his latent and insidious attack upon the freedom of English trade, if not on the existence of Englishmen in the country. But when he proceeded to action, the weak side of his policy, whenever matured, disclosed itself. He had not overrated his influence with the native, but he had underrated the resistance which its exercise was to elicit from the European; and having forced the English, in self-defence, into the service of his Indian opponents, he soon found that he must battle for life and death with our countrymen, who slowly, but surely, taking their sides, and animated by Clive's spirit, and enlightened by his genius, displayed in the later stages of the contest an energy and determination equal to his own.

The European peace left Dupleix in a favorable position for entering on his great design. He had 2,000 European soldiers, almost double that number of sepoys, artillery in plenty and of good quality, several competent officers, a strongly fortified capital, improved credit, and the high and well-earned fame of his late splendid achievement. And the opportunity which he coveted soon occurred. Chunda Sahib, son-in-law of Anwarodeen's predecessor, had in old days been on good terms with the French, and was personally known to the Governor-General. But he had long languished in a Mahratta prison, whence Dupleix now procured his release, and encouraged him to assert his right to the Carnatic succession. About the same time the great viceroy of the Dekkan, Nizam ul Mulk, died ; and Mirzapha Jung, a son of his daughter, claimed, by his grandfather's appointment, to succeed him, in supersession of Nazir Jung, the Nizam's second son, the eldest being permanently employed at Delhi. Mirzapha obtained little support: he was defeated, and fled southward. But Chunda Sahib, an able soldier, an experienced politician, and a man of vigorous character, now made common cause with him. The two pretenders invaded the Carnatic; and, being energetically opposed by the Nawab, preferred a joint request for assistance to the ruler of Pondicherry. Great concessions to the French were offered; and the momentous bargain was soon struck.

The French contingent consisted of 400 Europeans and 1,200 sepoys, with six field-pieces, commanded by Count D'Autheuil, a sturdy veteran, but of no great capacity, and afflicted with the gout. Dupleix announced the step to the directors, justifying it principally on the ground that it was to be recompensed by the cession to the company of Villenore and a district around that town, which would yield a considerable revenue. Chunda Sahib was to furnish provisions, transport, etc., and the troops were to draw pay, as usual, from Pondicherry.

The allied army found Anwarodeen entrenched in a very strong position. The French attacked vehemently, but were repulsed; a second attack, led by D'Autheuil in person, also failed, and he was disabled. Bussy, a young officer destined to become very famous, now took the command, and stormed the entrenchments. Anwarodeen was killed, and his army cut up and dispersed. The allies entered Arcot in triumph; and there Mirzapha was proclaimed subahdar of the Dekkan, and appointed Chunda Sahib Nawab of the Carnatic. Then they marched to Pondicherry, where Dupleiz gave them a magnificent reception, and spared no pains to impress them by the assumption of viceregal state, and a full muster of his formidable troops.

With military insight he then insisted on the immediate reduction of Trichinopoly and Gingee. The maritime province, besides its intrinsic importance, was an indispensable base for operations in the Dekkan. The late victory had left the Carnatic without a ruler, and, following so soon after the successful defence of Pondicherry, had spread a general terror of the French arms. The English as yet made no sign of opposition to Dupleix's bold game ; indeed, they were willing to recognize Chunda Sahib's title. Nazir Jung was hovering above the Ghauts, and his threatened approach made it advisable to lose no time in securing the military occupation of the lower country. Gingee was a very strong fortress in the interior of the Carnatic. Trichinopoly, in the basin of the Cavery, was strongly fortified, and a place of great political importance as a sort of second capital of the Carnatic, and of no less military consequence with a view to assuring the fidelity of Tanjore, and the wilder regions further to the south. It was also a barrier toward Mysore. Mahomed Ali, a younger son of Anwarodeen, had fled thither, and seemed disposed to make a stand as claimant of the nawabship. But fear of the English checked the progress of Mirzapha and Chunda Sahib. Till Boscawen left the coast they dallied at Arcot. Then, having received from Dupleix a *lac* of rupees, 800 French and 300 sepoys, with a siege train, under M. Duquesne, they began their march. But instead of attacking Trichinopoly they entered Tanjore, bent on rifling that rich principality. The Rajah was a Mahratta, a collateral descendant of Sivaji ; and he cunningly kept them in play for months, until Dupleix's patience was exhausted, and he ordered the French commander to storm the capital. An attack was made on the outworks and upon a gate of the city. Then the Rajah came to terms, and agreed to pay a large contribution. But by tendering obsolete coins, and plate and jewels of questionable value, he contrived to delay the settlement until his object was gained; and the invaders were suddenly appalled by the tidings that Nazir Jung, at the head of an immense army, had entered the Carnatic. The English also had begun, timidly and sparingly, to reinforce Mahomed Ali and the Tanjore prince. The allied chiefs broke up their camp and retreated, baffled, discredited, and dejected, to Pondicherry.

Nazir, of course, espoused Mahomed Ali's cause, and was promptly joined by an English contingent under Major Lawrence, a capable and experienced officer. The Madras government, at this time, certainly acted rather from the instinct of self-preservation than from deliberate policy. Dupleix's insinuation, we may add, that the junction of this contingent was due simply to heavy bribes received by Lawrence and his officers, is gratuitous and absurd. And though he affected to laugh at the impertinence of "two lieutenants declaring war on the king of France," he was fully alive to his dangerous position. The forces of his allies did not exceed 8,000 men; his own small army might be outnumbered by the English; while Nazir's host was estimated at 300,000. But he hoped that fear would restrain the natives, and political considerations the English, from attacking Pondicherry; and he relied on his own diplomatic ability for effecting a compromise, or, if Nazir proved intractable, for circumventing him. Thus he boldly arrayed his troops outside the city, and engaged in negotiation. He seems to have thought that he might induce Nazir to confer the Carnatic on one of his allies and an extensive appanage in the Dekkan on the other. Thus, could he detach Nizam ul Mulk's son from the English, and make him his friend, his own influence would be paramount in southern India.

Meanwhile he advised a night attack, in the hope of terrifying Nazir, and bringing him to reason. D'Autheuil adopted the suggestion: Nazir retreated in alarm and seemed disposed to come to terms; when a large party of French officers, whether from cupidity and disappointment at finding the service more arduous and less lucrative than they had anticipated, or from actual cowardice, suddenly mutinied; in the face of the enemy resigned their commissions, and sneaked off to Pondicherry, where Dupleix met the dastards at the gate and placed them in strict confinement. D'Autheuil was obliged to retreat, and fought his way back, gallantly covered by Chunda Sahib and his cavalry; but Mirzapha in despair threw himself on his uncle's mercy, and contrary to promise was imprisoned and fettered.

This catastrophe for a time prostrated Dupleix. But the strains of his harp are said to have soothed him; and his wife's tidings that Mirzapha was still alive and that his imprisonment was much resented by several of Nazir's principal supporters, roused him to renewed exertion. He resolved to maintain an unflinching attitude, to demand the same terms as before, to recognize Nazir as subahdar, but to insist on his releasing his nephew and making either him or Churda Sahib Nawab of the Carnatic with the appanage of Adoni for the other. And through his agents and in a letter to Nazir, he appealed to every motive that he thought likely to influence the prince; promising, in case the English contingent were dismissed, or retired, to contrib‥te double or even treble the number of French soldiers for the subahdar's service. The negotiation lingered; then Dupleix broke it off, and ordered another attack on Nazir's camp, who thereupon retreated in unseemly haste to Arcot; and Lawrence, finding him impracticable, led his men back to Fort St. David.

Dupleix employed the respite thus gained partly in secret attempts to undermine the fidelity of Nazir's adherents, partly in bold operations against Mahomed Ali, who was encamped on the banks of the river near Fort St. David. A French force under D'Autheuil suddenly occupied the pagoda of Trivadi, which in such hands was equivalent to a strong fortress; and an attempt to recover it made by Mahomed Ali, assisted by the English and a large detachment of Nazir's troops, was repulsed. Then, as before, the English quarreled with their employer, and left him. Dupleix largely reinforced D'Authueil, and ordered him to attack Mahomed Ali's army, which was routed with great slaughter, and with hardly any loss to the French. Nazir took little heed, and amused himself with hunting and less respectable pleasures.

Circumstances now favored the move which Dupleix had long contemplated, the acquisition of Gingee. Bussy spontaneously submitted to him a plan of attack, which was approved, and its execution intrusted to the projector. From the plain shot up a massive eminence, on which was the *pettah*, or town, its walls following the irregularities of the hill. The summit broke into three peaks, each surmounted by a separate citadel. The whole was strongly garrisoned, well supplied with artillery, and well provisioned, and was believed by the natives to be impregnable. But Bussy knew his business, and was no carpet knight. The wreck of Mahomed Ali's army had here found refuge, and thus sheltered might have baffled the young commander. But, with incredible folly, these already beaten troops were led out to battle in the plain below; were, of course, again routed, and pursued up the hill; and the victors nearly succeeded in entering the town along with them. One of the gates was blown open; and after an obstinate contest in the streets, the town was won toward nightfall. No time was lost in assailing the citadels. Bussy formed his men in three columns, himself leading the attack on the principal work; and, in spite of the acclivity, of the strong defences, and of a murderous fire, before sunrise the French flag waved over the three crests of Gingee the impregnable.

D'Autheuil had come up to Bussy's support in the crisis of the batttle, and Dupleix urged him to advance at once on Arcot, where Nazir, loitering away his time in pleasure, quarrelling with his nobles, becoming every day more unpopular, and amazed at the rapid operations of the French, offered a tempting prey. But the monsoon was raging in its full fury; the country was almost impassable; D'Autheuil was old, gouty, and unenterprising; and he halted, deaf to Dupleix's reiterated appeals —*de faire l'impossible, et d'aller de l'avant.* Neither yet knew that Nazir was already seeking an accommodation. He betrayed his fears by demanding a suspension of arms, and of D'Autheuil's march on Arcot. This Dupleix refused, and insisted haughtily on his previous terms. But D'Autheuil's halt lulled the envoys and their master into fatal security, and encouraged them to protract the negotiation.

Meanwhile the disaffected nawabs of Canoul, Cudapah and Savanore instigated the French governor to order an attack on the subahdar's camp, promising to coöperate, and, if necessary, to secure his person. All they asked for themselves was a French flag, the hoisting of which would prevent a collision between their own troops and the assailants. Dupleix readily complied; gave the flag, and confided his intention to D'Autheuil and to La Touche, who was to command the party. Nazir became more and more uneasy and undecided. He meditated retreating to the Dekkan, but was deterred by the disaffected nobles. At last he sent to accept Dupleix's terms. But in the interval La Touche had been ordered to advance. The French attacked; the traitors drew off their forces, and ranged them apart; Nazir, slowly convinced that he had stooped in vain to conciliate an implacable adversary, strove as vainly to check the progress of the assailants. In the bitterness of his heart he rode up to and reviled the Nawab of Canoul, who replied by sending a bullet through his heart. Mirzapha, who had been ordered for execution at the beginning of the affray, was liberated by the conspirators, proclaimed subahdar, and paraded in state, preceded by the ghastly trophy of his uncle's head exalted on a pole. Bussy met him fresh from the battlefield, and typified too plainly the alien influence to which he owed his sudden deliverance and precarious elevation.

Elated by the success of his policy, Dupleix prepared to take full advantage of this abrupt revolution. His first care was to make arrangements for enthroning Mirzapha at Pondicherry, with every circumstance that could give luster to the occasion, and significance to his own weight in the political scale. A vast and gorgeous tent was erected, within which were placed two chairs of state (or "thrones" as M. Hamont calls them), one for Mirzapha, the other for the Viceroy and Governor-General. Mirzapha first entered the tent and seated himself, encircled by the Dekkan nobles in all their finery. Dupleix advanced to the rendezvous in an imposing procession. He did homage to Mirzapha, and, tendering the customary *nuzzur*, was installed by him on the vacant chair of state. Then the native grandees in turn saluted and presented tokens of reverence to the viceroy of the king of France and Mogul Nawab by imperial appointment. Dupleix was invested with the *khelat*—a splendid robe of state, once the gift of the great emperor Aurungzib to Mirzapha's ancestor—together with a turban, a sash, a sword, shield, and dagger; and he paraded throughout the day in these emblematical appendages of oriental dignity. His grateful ally formally declared him nawab of all India south of the Kistna; bestowed on him a pompous name, indicative of valor and assured victory; raised him to the rank of a commander of 7,000 horsemen; and added the more substantial donations of the town and territory of Valdore, to be held by him and his descendants, and of a large annuity to himself, and another of equal value to his wife. The subahdar moreover decreed that the money of Pondicherry should have exclusive currency in southern India; acknowledged the sovereignty of the French company over Masulipatam and Yanoon; and enlarged their territory at Karikal. He is said also to have formally announced that all petitions to himself should be thenceforth preferred through Dupleix.

Such a scene and such treatment may well have turned the Frenchman's head, and exposed him to the half incredulous, half admiring ridicule of his lively countrymen, and to the serious envy and bitter taunts of his crestfallen English rivals. But, vain as he may have been, he knew too well the precarious character of his exaltation, the serious difficulties that lay before him in the way of consolidating his equivocal and hybrid dominion, and securing the solid acquisitions which accompanied the grant of empty titles, and the foppish adornments in which he masqueraded. And though he played his part with becoming gravity as a native potentate, his next move was dictated by sober policy. Professing his deep gratitude for the ample favors conferred on him, he disclaimed all wish to become a personal Indian ruler: he had but obeyed the orders of the emperor in suppressing rebellion, and maintaining the cause of the rightful subahdar. But in this good work Chunda Sahib had been equally faithful and zealous. Let him, therefore, retain the prize that was his due, and which he had contemplated when he cemented the alliance between Mirzapha and the French. Let him be confirmed in the Nawabship of the Carnatic. The proposal was adopted. Chunda Sahib's effective assistance in defending the province was secured; while the ingenious Frenchman prudently retained the title of sub-viceroy of India south of the Kistna, which gave him formal supremacy over Chunda and might on occasion be usefully employed in diplomatic disputes with the English. Lastly, to confirm and perpetuate the impression produced by the incidents of this great day, he ordered a triumphal column to be erected on the site of Nazir Jung's overthrow. And around it was to arise a city whose name was to commemorate the same event, and his capital share in it.

In the midst of his triumph, Dupleix realized that he must pay a perilous price for the maintenance of his influence with the subahdar. Mirzapha was anxious to return to the Dekkan; and he urgently requested that a body of French troops might escort him, and continue in his service. This request was quite in accordance with Dupleix's general policy; but in his actual circumstances it was premature. The small number of his European soldiers, and especially of officers, and the danger of diminishing them while Mahomed Ali was still master of Trichinopoly, and the attitude of the English uncertain, were very serious considerations. And it was too likely that those who had already been adverse to his intervention in native disputes, would strongly disapprove of this remote diversion of troops intended to guard the French possessions on the coast. Thus the difficulties that he raised do not seem to have been simply effected. But Mirzapha's lavish promises were very seductive, and Mahomed Ali determined him by offering to surrender Trichinopoly, if he should be allowed to retain his father's treasures, and receive an appanage in the Dekkan. He reported the transaction to the directors with a request for a strong reinforcement, and the intimation that both the native rulers were to pay the troops while in their service.

Bussy was appointed to attend Mirzapha with 300 French soldiers, including ten officers, 2,000 sepoys and Caffres, and a battery of artillery. Dupleix was much affected at their departure. His anxiety was increased by the consciousness that Mirzapha was already in a critical position. The three nawabs who had conspired against Nazir were so exorbitant in their demands on the gratitude of his successor, that he was equally unable and unwilling to satisfy them. The favors lavished on Dupleix made them still more dissatisfied; and though at the center of French power they had confined themselves to complaints, at a distance these might ripen into violent acts. This misgiving was soon realized. As the army traversed Cudapah, the territory of one of the malcontents, they created a commotion, in which they were worsted and slain. But at the close of the contest Mirzapha was shot down. Thus, what Dupleix had gained in a moment by the murder of Nazir, was as suddenly, and by the same savage agency, imperiled by the slaughter of Mirzapha. But he now profited by his skillful selection of instruments. Bussy and his Brahmin adviser procured the provisional exaltation of Salabat Jung, a younger brother of Nazir, and who was in the camp, Mirzapha's infant son being rejected as ineligible at such a crisis. Dupleix highly approved of an arrangement which promised so well for the maintenance of his influence in the upper country. The new subahdar was acknowledged by all parties; and his first act was to confirm and extend the benefactions granted by his predecessor to the French. The army resumed its march; and Bussy and his contingent prosecuted an adventurous and glorious career, which lies beyond our immediate scope. But we may mention that it did not terminate, nor French ascendency cease in the Dekkan, until Lally hastily recalled Bussy to the Carnatic; and Forde, detached by Clive from Bengal, routed the French at Peddapore, stormed Masulipatam, and conquered the northern Circars.

Hitherto Dupleix's policy seemed justified by its results. He had humbled the English and exalted the French by the capture of Madras, and the sucessful defence of Pondicherry. He had dispelled the awe of native armaments, and with a handful of men had asserted the resistless superiority of European skill and discipline over Asiastic numbers.

The English, dazzled by the splendor of his achievements, disheartened at their own poor performance in the rapid drama, mistrustful of Mahomed Ali, and knowing the aversion of the directors to the perils and expenses of war, seemed little inclined to dispute the progress of their bold rival. Still Trichinopoly was not surrendered.

Mahomed Ali's overtures had been a mere expedient for gaining time. He had now, by lavish promises, secured the assistance of the Mysore regent, of a Mahratta force, and of the English; and he flatly refused to evacuate Trichinopoly. Its siege was first undertaken by D'Autheuil; but an attack of gout in errupted his construction of batteries, and disabled him so completely that Dupleix recalled him and in an evil hour gave the command to Law, a nephew of the great speculator. By a curious coincidence, the timidity of the nephew was destined to prove as fatal to French ambition in Asia, as the uncle's audacity had proved to her financial affairs in Europe. The younger Law was by no means destitute of assurance; he was voluble and plausible at Pondicherry; he had shown himself brave in the defence of the fort of Ariancopan; but he was utterly unfit for a separate and critical command. In such a position he was oppressed with the sense of responsibility; and from first to last his desponding temper and hesitating conduct went far to bring about the ensuing catastrophe. His first dispatch must have given Dupleix a painful shock. He described the place as too strong to be taken by a *coup de main;* he dwelt on the difficulties of a regular siege, and the loss of life that must attend the final assault, and recommended a close blockade as the easiest and safest plan. Dupleix thought otherwise; but he was at the time prostrated by the death of his brother, his one devoted champion against the libels of Labourdonnais, and the growing disfavor with which his policy was regarded in France. Thus, against his better judgment, he yielded to Law's importunity, and consented to the blockade.

From this moment Fortune seemed to have deserted her spoiled child. Hitherto the generalship had been on his side. Now this was reversed. Clive suddenly appeared on the scene; created a powerful diversion by taking and heroically defending Arcot, the capital of the Carnatic; assumed the offensive in turn, and defeated his besiegers in a bloody battle; and on their retreat to Gingee prepared to relieve

Trichinopoly. Dupleix sought to gain time for the operation of the blockade by threatening Madras, and amusing Clive with marches, and countermarches. But the "heaven-born general" was not to be thus dallied with innocuously. He overtook the French army at Covrepauk, and inflicted on it another terrible defeat. He then hurried off to expedite a convoy for the relief of the beleaguered city, demolishing on his way Dupleix's vaunting column. The spell of French invincibility was broken; the military reputation of the English was established; an able general, at the head of a victorious army, was marching to the critical point; the covering army, which ought to have disputed his advance, was dissipated; and to crown all, Law chose this appropriate moment for requesting leave to revisit Pondicherry, on account of his wife's approaching confinement. Dupleix refused, and rebuked him sharply. He ought to have superseded him, but was at a loss for a fit man to replace him; and he hoped, by positive and minute orders, to keep the malingerer up to his work.

To intercept the convoy was of the utmost importance; and Law's greatly superior force ought to have made this a comparatively easy task, considering the long train of cumbrous wagons, slow oxen, and timid coolies, the distance to be traversed, and the natural obstacles on the way. He had 900 Europeans, 2,000 sepoys, and Chunda Sahib's army, computed at 20,000. These Dupleix reinforced with every available man from the garrison of Gingee. The English had only 400 Europeans and 900 sepoys. Law was ordered to leave 300 French and two-thirds of Chunda's multitude before the place, and with the rest to meet the convoy as far in advance as possible. After promising compliance, he veered round; enlarged on the danger of a Mahratta inroad; suggested a march into Mysore to counteract it; and finally proposed to withdraw his whole army into the island. Dupleix, amazed and indignant, in a biting dispatch insisted that the last hopeful project should be submitted to a council of war, confident that the general voice of the officers would condemn it. Thus he concluded: *Laissez l'avenir venir et Balladji-Rao* [*i. e.*, the Peishwa]. *Ne songez qu'au présent; tachez de vous persuader de l'importance de détruire le convoi; laissez moi le soin du reste.* And announcing that the English army had left Cuddalore, he repeated his prophetic warning: *Il est de votre honneur de détruire le secours. Tout dépend de ce coup. Ne négligez rien pour réussir.* But Law seemed fascinated by Clive's terrible audacity, energy, and skill, now all the more formidable because they were combined with Lawrence's experience, and respectable though less original military talents. While he should have been marching, he was still arguing; and Dupleix's crushing replies die away in a wail of indignant despondence. *Je vous avertis de tout; qu'en arriverat-il? Dieu le sait. J'y suis résigné, et ce que j'apprendrai ne me surprendra plus. Il sera pourtant difficile de persuader en France que trente mille hommes en aient laissé passer deux mille, embarrassés d'un charroi et d'un transport effroyables.*

Thus Lawrence, who had now taken the chief command, neared Coiladdy unopposed. Thence he was fired upon with some loss and more confusion; and a bold sally from the fort, supported by an advance from the French lines, must have been perilous, if not fatal, to his immediate object. But Law recalled the garrison of Coiladdy, and, fearing a sally from the city, posted his army so awkwardly that Lawrence succeeded in *turning* it. By a resolute onslaught during this flank march Law might have defeated the English, or at least taken or destroyed a large part of the stores and provisions. But he hesitated too long; and when he did advance he was daunted by a sortie of the garrison, and after an idle cannonade fell back. Meanwhile the convoy had pursued its way on the unexposed flank of the English column, and was triumphantly welcomed in the city.

This decisive failure completed the prostration of the Scotchman's spirit. Dupleix's Cassandra warnings must have rung in his ears like the knell of his fortune and honor as a soldier. Taking counsel of his fears—and *not*, as Dupleix had expressly ordered, of his officers—he gave the word for an immediate retreat into the island. This decision was vigorously, but fruitlessly, combated by Chunda Sahib. And it was carried out in indecent and prodigal haste. A large part of the vast stores of provisions which had been laid in was sacrificed, together with much of the baggage. Chunda Sahib gloomily followed. The French occupied the pagoda of Jumbakishna: of their allies some went into Seringham; others settled themselves along the bank of the Coleroon.

Dupleix described his heart as "bleeding" at these tidings, which at first he refused to believe. When convinced, he resolved, too late, to supersede the craven general. *Je ne veux plus être prophète, j'ai trop averti en vain. Il faut retirer le commandement à cet homme.* He earnestly appealed to the infirm but gallant D'Autheuil to undertake the arduous, perhaps desperate, task of saving the army and its honor. And D'Autheuil, like Coote in similar circumstances, responded to the call of duty. In announcing to Law his recall, Dupleix added the cutting gibe: *Je suis persuadé que cet arrangement va faire plaisir à madame votre femme, qui ne désire que le moment de vous tenir dans ses bras.*

Meanwhile Clive had proposed a plan which could hardly fail to bring the contest to a rapid and decisive issue. His aim was to isolate the enemy in their exposed situation; and thus, as at Syracuse, to turn the besiegers into the besieged. One division of the army was to guard the city, and threaten Law from the south; another was to push across the rivers, intercept his communication with Pondicherry, and operate against any reinforcement which Dupleix might be able to provide. Though he proposed that the two divisions should remain within a forced march of each other, Clive's project was, considering the disparity of numbers, a characteristically bold one; as Orme says: "This was risking the whole to save the whole." Lawrence assented, and gave the command of the detachment to Clive himself. He soon occupied Semiaveram, seven miles north of the Coleroon. Dupleix insisted that he should be immediately assailed and dislodged. But Law, already in want of provisions, threw away his last chance of profiting by his superior numbers, and of securing the junction of D'Autheuil, who might still have rescued him. Nor was this all. He had already engrossed and paralyzed almost all the soldiers of the French army. He now opened a correspondence with the enemy, still more deeply depressed his troops, and their allies, and excited suspicion of treasonable intentions. Dupleix authorized D'Autheuil, in the last extremity, to conclude peace, which was to be made formally between Chunda Sahib and Mahomed Ali. *La situation*, he added, *où l'aridité de Law a mis nos affaires me font penser que c'est le seul parti qui nous reste.* Thus he seems to have suspected that Law, like his uncle, was making his own game at the expense of his adopted country. Though this imputation may be dismissed, it was less ridiculous than a wild project which the governor-general broached of liberating the army by bribing Lawrence.

D'Autheuil's force, including the garrison of Volcondah, which he picked up on his way, amounted only to 120 Europeans, 500 sepoys, and four guns, with a large convoy. He sent a letter, in duplicate, to announce his approach, and request Law to detach to his support. One copy of the letter was safely received; but the other Clive intercepted, and thereupon advanced against D'Autheuil, who retreated hastily. Law sent a feeble party to Semiaveram in Clive's absence, but on his unexpected return he overpowered it; and, after more fighting and the capture of the convoy at Utatoor, he fell upon D'Autheuil at Volcondah and compelled him to surrender.

Before this happened the monsoon had burst, and increased the difficulty of crossing the swelling rivers. But while Chunda Sahib's army, as his fortune declined, dwindled away apace, and many of his followers joined the English, Lawrence made his way into the island; threw up an entrenchment across it from north to south; and the Tanjore troops being posted to the east, and the Mysoreans to the west, of the city, while Clive's division lined the north bank of the Coleroon, the toils were effectually thrown round the late besiegers. Dupleix still maintained that famine would be no excuse for surrender, and urged Law to fight his way to Karikal, which he thought practicable, as the flooded river would prevent the junction of the English divisions. As it was, Law showed no disposition to make the desperate effort, but, on 13th June, 1752, tamely capitulated; and with him 35 officers, 785 Europeans, 2,000 sepoys, and 41 guns were captured. Chunda Sahib gave himself up to Monacjee, the Tanjorine general, who put him to death.

Dupleix's position might now well appear desperate; to make peace at once, or to recall Bussy and employ him in a supreme effort to capture Trichinopoly, seemed the only alternative open to him. Yet he chose neither, but preferred to try a third plan, for which there was certainly much to be said, but which involved the proverbial danger of a middle course, and proved in the end most unfortunate.

He despaired of obtaining tolerable terms from an enemy flushed with such a victory. He calculated that political caution would restrain the English from an immediate attack on the French capital, and he did not fear such an attack if made by native forces only. He had also reason to believe that the victors were on the eve of a quarrel among themselves, which he might turn to his advantage. Reinforcements from France were due; and they arrived opportunely. Clive's health too was impaired, and he returned to Europe. To him the English had mainly owed their success, and without him they would be much less formidable. Moreover, Dupleix hoped to form a league between the Subahdar and the Peishwa, who had lately been at war; to bring down the united forces of the Dekkan on Mysore, so as to compel the regent of that state to espouse the French cause; and then to make this great confederation available for reducing Trichinopoly, overpowering the English and Mahomed Ali, and restoring his own ascendency in the Carnatic. Whatever force there might be in some of these reasons for persevering in the contest, the scheme of native cooperation from the Dekkan, the magnitude and comprehensiveness of which excite M. Hamont's glowing admiration, required too much time to give it effect: it was also too complicated; it ignored too much the jealous and vindictive position of the Poona Mahrattas; and it was promptly thwarted by one of the Nizam's ministers, who stirred up a mutiny in his army, which prevented its taking the field, and was the prelude of other serious and engrossing disturbances.

We have not space to follow the course of the renewed war, which was equally notable for the hard fighting of the Europeans on both sides; for the steadfastness and wariness of Dalton, the commander in Trichinopoly, which again became the chief bone of contention; for the activity of Lawrence in relieving the beleaguered city, and his skill in defeating with his small army the vast hosts of the assailants; and, above all, for the indefatigable efforts of Dupleix to supply the means of carrying on the obstinate contest, and to repair, by his judicious and detailed instructions, the conspicuous want of capacity among his officers.

The diplomacy of Dupleix, or rather that of his wife, detached the Mysorean and Morari Rao from Mahomed Ali and the English; and securing them as allies, reëstablished the blockade of the city. But as he was never able to take it, and the wasting war involved him and the company deeper and deeper in embarrassment and increased the exasperation of the English against him, there seemed less and less hope that he could escape condemnation for persisting in designs which, however plausible in their origin, were opposed by the stern logic of facts. Thus he did at last consent to treat, but, even then, in no temper of practical compromise. He still insisted on the recognition by his adversaries of the authority which had been delegated to him by successive subahdars; and supported his pretensions by alleged charters from them, and from the emperor, which the English loudly asserted to be forgeries. This charge was vehemently repudiated at the time by the French negotiators. But thus no common basis could be established; and hostilities were resumed. The end, however, was at hand. In this last transaction Dupleix seems to have been almost judicially blind; for relating the conference to Bussy, he writes: *Tout ce que nous avons présenté, firmans, paravanas, et autres pièces, tout avait été forgé par nous.* This is a melancholy revelation, though not more so than Clive's shamelessly fraudulent treatment of Omichund.

The storm that had long been brewing in France was now to burst on Dupleix's devoted head. The Governor-General must, indeed, have been well aware that he stood on very slippery ground; that powerful influences were banded together against him; that the surrender of the French army at Trichinopoly had gone far to eclipse the luster of earlier achievements; and that his subsequent failure to reduce that city was an unanswerable argument against his policy. The company resented the suspension of their trade, and the absorption of their funds in war expenses. The ministers were anxious to conciliate England, and feared that the Carnatic struggle might provoke a European war. Public opinion was adverse to schemes which seemed at once visionary and inglorious in their results. Labourdonnais was indefatigable in fanning the flame of indignation against his rival; and Dupleix's champion, D'Autheuil, whom he had sent home to explain and defend his course, was so injudicious in his advocacy, that M. Hamont says of him roundly: *Son ambassade fut plus nuisible qu'utile aux intérêts de Dupleix.*

Thus negotiations were entered into with England, and a convention was concluded, whereby commissioners were to be appointed for reconciling the two Companies, and preventing the recurrence of war between them while their respective nations should be at peace. And it was agreed that both Dupleix and Saunders should be recalled. To estimate this point rightly, we must look back at Dupleix's conduct, and remember his characteristic disposition. Did he act wisely in taking up Chunda Sahib's cause. If so—and this proceeding had been condoned by the directors—was he wise in prosecuting the was against Mahomed Ali and the English after the loss of his army and the death of his candidate? His reasons for doing so we have stated. But they did not satisfy his employers or the king's ministers; and as the continuation of the contest seemed to them to open an indefinite vista of expense and peril without any corresponding advantage, his recall appeared to them essential. For could he be trusted not only to effect, but to abide by, a real pacification? Would it not have been found too late, that, taking occasion from some new and plausible opening for adventure he had resumed the attempt to redevelop his "system?"

But whatever may be thought as to the necessity of his removal, there can be only one opinion of the way in which it was effected, and of the French commissioner's conduct toward him. It would seem that the Government and the Company were seriously afraid that one who had so long ruled as a master might refuse to relinquish his authority without a struggle. Godeheu was accordingly provided with 2,000 soldiers, a force that, if sent sooner and properly officered, might have brought the long contest to a triumphant issue. And an order signed by the king empowered Godeheu to arrest the Governor-General, guard him securely, and send him home a prisoner on the first vessel that should sail for France. This mandate was absolute. But a second order dispensed with its execution in case Dupleix should submit quietly; though it added, that if Godeheu judged it necessary to arrest him, Madame Dupleix and her daughter were to share the same fate, and were to have no communication with him. Meanwhile the dispatches of the directors, and Godeheu's own letters, were so worded as to excite no surmise of the real drift of the commission. So completely was Dupleix deceived, that he wrote thus: *N'allez pas regarder cette résolution de la compagnie comme une marque de son ingratitude à mon égard. Je la regarde, au contraire, comme un service essentiel qu'elle me rend, et surtout à avoir fait le choix ce Godeheu, qui est le plus cher de mes amis.*

On arriving in the river the commissioner

sent another unctuous and cunningly reticent letter, declining, however, Dupleix's proffered hospitality. He disembarked surrounded by guards and other military display. The Governor-General met him on the bank, and offered him his hand. Godeheu bowed stiffly, and presented a letter from himself for Dupleix's perusal. This, amid many polite phrases, and still suppressing the occasion, and misrepresenting the character of the measure, abruptly revealed the fact of the Governor-General's recall, and that of his family, to France. *L'intention du roi*, said this glozing epistle, *n'est que de mettre la compagnie à porté de vos lumières.* Before Dupleix could recover from his astonishment, or ask any question, Godeheu produced the royal mandate revoking the Governor-General's commission, and a second, demanding a detailed report on the company's affairs. Dupleix calmly perused these documents but it was observed that he grew pale. Declaring his readiness to obey the king's commands, he requested to be favored with any other of which Godeheu might be the bearer. Then with one long-drawn sigh, and a fixed and contemptuous gaze at his false friend, he silently awaited the issue of this strange scene. Godeheu desired him to summon the Council. The news spread fast, and a crowd beset the precincts of the council chamber. Godeheu ordered his guards to disperse it. Then seating himself, and motioning Dupleix to sit beside him, he solemnly recited his instructions amid profound silence. Dupleix showed great self-restraint, but his hands at times twitched convulsively. With bowed head he listened attentively, and at the close he rose, and with extended arms exclaimed, *Vive le roi!* The cry was taken up, and he quitted the council chamber, and poured forth to Bussy the bitterness of his soul.

The following evening Godeheu assumed command as governor. But his moral authority was impaired by the subterfuge which he had practiced, and by the pitiful contrast which he presented to the brilliant and undaunted ruler who had so long defied the storms of fate, and whose attitude of dignified resignation might imply tacit rebuke, but offered no excuse for violence. The new governor complained that Dupleix talked of returning in the course of two years. But as he had himself, by his misrepresentation, suggested this hope, so he now determined to frustrate it. He sought eagerly, but vainly, to ruin Dupleix's personal character by eliciting against him charges of pecuniary corruption; and regretted that, to facilitate this noble end, the order of arrest had not been left absolute. *C'était le moyen de découvrir tout, et de me mettre en état d'agir avec fruit.* In default of this expedient he imprisoned Papiapoule, the agent who managed the assignments on the Carnatic districts, mortgaged to Dupleix for the liquidation of his large *personal* advances to the native princes. This tyrannical act not producing any incriminating revelations, he misappropriated the assignments to the use of the Company; refused, on the absurd plea of their intricacy, to sanction the auditing and passing of the Governor-General's accounts which showed a balance against the company of a quarter of a million sterling; and even prevented the cashing of a large bill which they had made payable to Dupleix. Thus this false and cruel man reduced his old benefactor and recently alleged intimate friend to beggary and worse; for Dupleix's influence had induced many friends and admirers to intrust him with large sums for the public service, which he thus lost the means of repaying, and for which he was sued on his return to France. Nor would Godeheu advance him money on the Company's account and on the security of his claims; though he privately lent him a small sum, which the ex-governor-general was constrained to accept for immediate necessities.

The commissioner's political adjustment is beyond our present province. But we may remark generally, that although later orders from France preserved the Dekkan connection, the tendency of his other arrangements was to sacrifice the interests of his countrymen, and to give England a decided preponderance on the eastern coast. Thus he aggravated the unfavorable conditions under which Lally contended with us a few years later, and may be said to have prepared the way for the downfall of the French power in India.

The melancholy close of Dupleix's story may be told very briefly. He embarked amid the cordial and publicly expressed sympathy of the settlement. His arrival in France was greeted with popular enthusiasm; at first he was well received by the ministers; and the Pompadour made much of his wife. He even began to hope that he might be reinstated. But the pacification once accomplished, he was frowned upon by the court, slighted by the ministry, harassed by creditors, insulted by officers formerly under his authority, and who had conceived grudges against him, and exposed to popular ridicule as a political charlatan. But worst of all was his treatment by his old employers. He could obtain no adjudication of his claims on the Company. In vain he memorialized, earnestly, luminously, convincingly. He was answered, and replied with indisputable cogency. The literary controversy was prolonged, but without effect. Godeheu's maneuver had encouraged and enabled the directors to evade a judicial settlement of his demands. And they were never settled.

The death of Madame Dupleix in November, 1756, left her husband unspeakably desolate. And though two years later he remarried, apparently happily, his second wife had little fortune, and he became more and more impoverished, though he still made gallant effort to relieve friends who had been involved in his ruin. He was at last threatened with an execution on his poor effects, and expulsion from his humble retreat. In a state of extreme exhaustion, he composed a last and piteous summary of his services, his wrongs, and his forlorn condition; and three days afterward he expired, on November 10, 1763, having survived the final triumph of the English in the great duel which he had first provoked. That Dupleix was not only a remarkable, but a really great man, is the general impression conveyed by an attentive study of his history. The originality, boldness and magnitude of his political conceptions; his versatile ability, displayed alike in its application to commerce, politics, and war; his inexhaustible fertility of resource; his high moral courage; his indomitable energy and perseverance; his munificent devotion of an ample fortune to the public service; the marvels which he wrought with inadequate means and unpromising instruments; the unhesitating confidence which he inspired both in Europeans and natives, and which was exemplified in the continuous acquiescence of his council in his adventurous policy; the admiration which he extorted from his enemies; the enthusiastic sympathy which he kindled not only in the young and chivalrous Bussy, but in the aged and gout-stricken D'Autheuil; the precautions which were adopted by the French authorities and their sycophantic agent to trepan and coerce him into the surrender of his authority; his loyal and unconditional submission to the adverse verdict, though it cast him down from the pinnacle of power under the feet of one of the meanest and most worthless of men; and his dignified demeanor after his resignation:—all these tokens bespeak the presence of a king of men.

He has been taxed with inordinate vanity. The charge, if not unfounded, seems to be at least much exaggerated, and mainly the result of misapprehension, national antipathy, personal prejudice, and studied misrepresentation. "Vain" was, nay is, one of the stock epithets too readily applied by sober Englishmen to their more mercurial and self-asserting neighbors; and it was, of course, liberally bestowed on one who pushed himself into such sudden and invidious eminence, and for a while bestrode the Indian world like a Colossus. And his policy of impressing the oriental imagination by a dramatic display of dignity as the French king's viceroy; by making much of the title of nawab to which he had succeeded, and parading the new honors and decorations received from his Mogul patron; and by trumpeting his successes far and wide, and graving in the living stone his triumph over Nazir Jung —all these devices naturally caused him to be regarded as a man of an unbounded stomach. This estimate was confirmed by his conduct in the later stages of the Carnatic contest. Orme mentions how, while Chunda Sahib was his tool, he provoked the English by setting up French flags round their territory, as if to warn them off from crossing *his* frontier. *Valeat quantum!* But is not British sensitiveness here as evident as French vanity? When, however, after Chunda Sahib's fall, Dupleix still refused to recognize Mahomed Ali, affected to give a title to Mortiz Ali, and at last produced a grant of the nawabship from the Subahdar to himself the monstrous assumption was most readily accounted for by the plausible theory, that the once lucky and now desperate adventurer was the dupe of his own extravagant conceit, which goaded him on to persevere in playing at kingship instead of "seeing things as they were," making peace and settling down to his proper business as the manager of a commercial concern. And Labourdonnais's aspersions fell in with this view of his rival's besotted egotism.

In spite of all this, we believe the charge to be substantially untrue, or at least unproved. To analyze correctly the mixed motives of human action, and to assign to each motive its relative strength, is never easy. But it is especially difficult when personal ambition and public views are intertwined; when the individual is the prime mover, and throughout the ruling agent, upon whose influence and reputation the success of an original and critical policy is staked; and when accordingly the exaltation of the man is essential to the execution of his designs. That Dupleix was public-spirited in his aims, that he was zealously devoted to the interests of the Company as he understood them, to the service of the king though that king was Louis XV., and to the glory and aggrandizement of his countrymen however little they understood him, we cannot doubt. How far personal considerations and feelings influenced him; how far his achievements and his barbaric honors stimulated his vanity, as they no doubt flattered his self-esteem; how far his personal claim to the *musnud* was put forward not only for public ends, but gratify a half-orientalized craving for high rank and swelling title—must remain uncertain.

Again, he has been sneered at as a physical coward; and Macaulay was not ashamed to repeat the silly sneer. That he did not lead armies in the field, is true enough: his business lay elsewhere. But a single incident which occurred during the siege of Pondicherry will be enough to clear up this point. Coming upon a group of soldiers, who were cowering before a shell that had just lighted among them, he approached, but too late to prevent the explosion, which, however, only covered him with dust and smoke. Turning to the men, he remarked coolly, *Vous voyez bien, enfants, que cela ne fait pas de mal.*

If the mature Governor-General did not, like the young factor Clive, turn soldier outright, his military capacity was shown in several ways. He was a great war minister. His promptitude, assiduity, and skill in making the most of his scanty resources and poor material, in organizing and equipping the various departments of the army, in improving the discipline and tone of the wretched recruits sent out from France, in raising and training sepoy corps, in pushing on his troops to the scene of action, employing them as effectively as circumstances permitted, and keeping them true, latterly, to a losing cause, will appear the more notable the more his story is studied in detail. Again, he was no mean master of the operations of war, both as a strategist and as a tactician. His insight was clear and comprehensive; his suggestions were generally apposite; his warnings too often prophetic. He insisted, from the first, on the extreme importance of reducing Trichinopoly and Gingee, and of the folly and danger of the Tanjore diversion. He consented most reluctantly, and against his judgment, to the first blockade of Trichinopoly; and at every stage of that fatal enterprise we have seen how well he understood the requirements of the position, and s rove by wise orders to check each approach to the catastrophé. In the course of the second blockade he ordered an escalade in the night, which very nearly succeeded. After Law's surrender, he was never strong enough to besiege the city in form. Though in his last campaigns he was overmatched throughout, his sagacious advice was most serviceable. He recommended that pitched battles in the open should be avoided; that the spade should be used more than the sword; that good positions, which he carefully selected and pointed out, should be occupied, and strongly entrenched with earthworks. And thus he was able to restore the confidence and supplement the scanty numbers of his own army to repulse with loss and disgrace to the English a formidable demonstration against Gingee, and to keep Lawrence himself at bay and inactive, until he was forced to hurry off to the relief of Trichinopoly, which was again on the verge of surrender for want of provisions.

Once more, Dupleix's defence of Pondicherry against Boscawen exhibits his military ability in yet another light. The plan of that defence was his own, the fruit (as we have already said) of his early devotion to the study of fortification; after Paradis's death he was entirely his own engineer: his zeal and confidence sustained the spirits, his skill directed the efforts, of the besieged; and with every allowance for the awkwardness of the besiegers the result seems to entitle him to a respectable place among military commanders.

It is unnecessary to dwell upon his proficiency in the diplomatic department of generalship, in which he was assisted by his wife, and which enabled him to rescue Pondicherry, to augment his small army with hosts of native allies, and after Chunda Sahib's death to detach the Mysoreans and Mahrattas from Mahomed Ali and the English, and with their aid to reëstablish the blockade of Trichinopoly. Thus, under the most serious and accumulating disadvantages, he continued to fight on, with varying fortune, unable to conquer, but still unconquered, until he fell, not by the arms of his antagonists in India, but by the arts of his opponents in France, the dextrous contrivance of the English negotiators, and the crushing dead-weight of a calamity which he had done all in his power to prevent, but of which he was doomed to pay the bitter penalty.

Dupleix was not only a great man, but in many respects a great statesman. His ruling idea of establishing European ascendency, in India, by a combination of martial enterprise and subsidiary relations with native rulers, and based partly on direct titular and territorial acquisitions from the Mogul or his deputies, partly on the indirect influence of the resources of western civilization, operating steadily as a sapping and transforming force on the disintegrated and discordant elements of native society, may, at the present day, seem obvious and almost commonplace. But not the less because experience has since proved that it was a practicable one, was it an original, subtle, and bold conception at the time. That Dupleix, so lightly equipped at the opening of his march, so grudgingly supported from his remote French base, so stoutly obstructed by the English, made such progress on the road to empire, and to the last guarded Pondicherry and Gingee intact, maintained the blockade of the second capital of the Carnatic, kept Bussy at Aurungabad, and thereby retained his influence over the subahdar, his reputation in the Dekkan as mayor of the palace, and his hold of the French possessions in the Circars, is surely enough to establish his pretensions to statesmanship, judging even by the vulgar test of accomplished results.

How much further he might have proceeded, had his heroic exertions been better sustained by his countrymen, and less stubbornly opposed by the British, may seem an idle question; yet in suggesting it we have, it appears to us, touched the blot that derogates from his fame as a practical and far-seeing statesman. He had a brilliant imagination, consummate dexterity, untiring energy, an indomitable will; but he seems to have lacked, as a politician, what, paradoxically enough, he so often displayed as a general—sobriety of judgment, the capacity or inclination to count the cost of his great undertaking before he entered on it, and again when, instead of making peace, he persevered in it, regardless of the warnings of experience. He knew that he owed his appointment to the improvement which he had effected in the Company's condition by a long course of *peaceful* enterprise.

He knew that the directors were so much

averse to military expenditure that, on the eve of war with England, they prescribed the most rigid economy in that respect, instead of sending reinforcements, and constrained him to fortify Pondicherry at his own cost. He knew that Madras had been reduced not by a regular armament from Europe, but by a nondescript force extemporized at the Isle of France; that Pondicherry had been preserved, first by an appeal to the Nawab, afterward by the clumsiness of the besiegers, and his own careful husbanding of a comparatively small army. This great success, and the subsequent hesitation of the English, might indeed tempt him to underrate them, and the danger of their interference with his designs. Still he knew well what Englishmen had been in the past, and might again show themselves—to his peril. He also knew well the intensity and sensitiveness of their commercial jealousy, the precariousness of native alliances, the uncertainties of war, the certainty that his policy of intervention, if tolerated by his employers for a while in a single case and in the full tide of startling success, would be disapproved as a general scheme, and in the case that had already occurred would be liable to condemnation on the first reverse, and to faint support in the interval. After Clive's rise and Lawrence's return to India, there could be no mistake as to the seriousness and potency of the English opposition. Law's disaster, so great in itself, so ominous in every way, was sure to be regarded as the fatal outcome of Dupleix's temerity. Whether, had he recalled Bussy to the Carnatic, and through him even succeeded in storming Trichinopoly, he could have recovered his ground, and concluded a favorable peace, seems doubtful; and not less so, whether the authorities in France would, after such a disaster, have allowed time for working out such a programme.

But Dupleix did *not* recall Bussy. The collapse in the Carnatic made him cling all the more tenaciously to the Dekkan. His "system" was at stake. The death of Chunda Sahib was an additional reason for adhering to the subahdar. The political legitimacy of Dupleix's attitude as a belligerent now depended entirely on Salabat Jung's sanction. He hoped also to receive material support from him, which was prevented by circumstances upon which we must not now enter, but which Dupleix ought to have taken into account. Yet without Bussy's help, without a single able officer, practically almost without an army of his own, and in desperate dependence on doubtful and treacherous native alliances, he neglected to make peace and thereby committed himself anew to a most precarious contest, which if not promptly and successfully ended, he must have been well aware, would in one way or another be his undoing. Such is hardly the conduct of a practical statesman. And, on the whole, the old estimate of Dupliex as a brilliant visionary; does not seem to be far from the truth; not, however, because he dreamed of what was impracticable in itself, but because he refused to discern the signs of the times, and to recognize the fact that what he coveted was, in his actual circumstances, beyond his reach. And we, who have since settled down in the promised land of his aspirations, ought to be the first to admit the great qualities, to speak gently of the defects, and to commiserate the misfortunes of the prophet, who impelled us to enter in and possess it.